30 Mixed Media Works

Richard Leach

ISBN: 978-1-365-69200-0

This book presents 30 pieces made between February 2015 and January 2017. They are reproduced at or near life size. The media include cardboard, glued paper, ink, pencil and crayon.

richardleach.deviantart.com

lulu.com/rleach

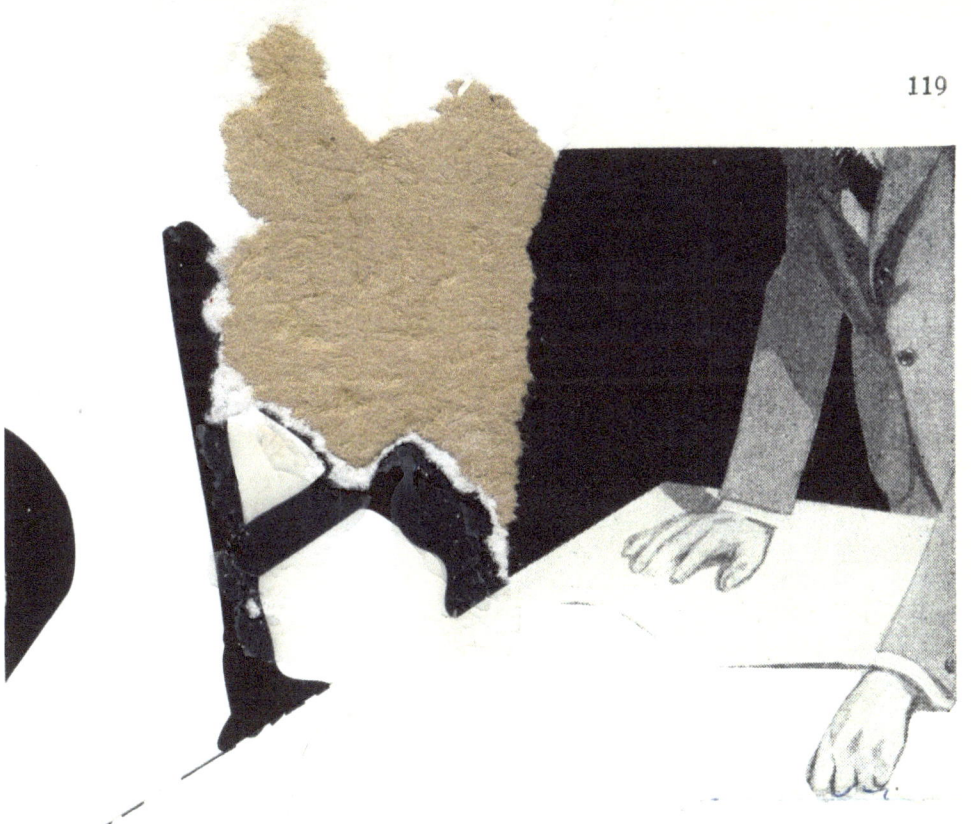

And mocking say, " $+123_{10} = +123 \times 10^{0}$

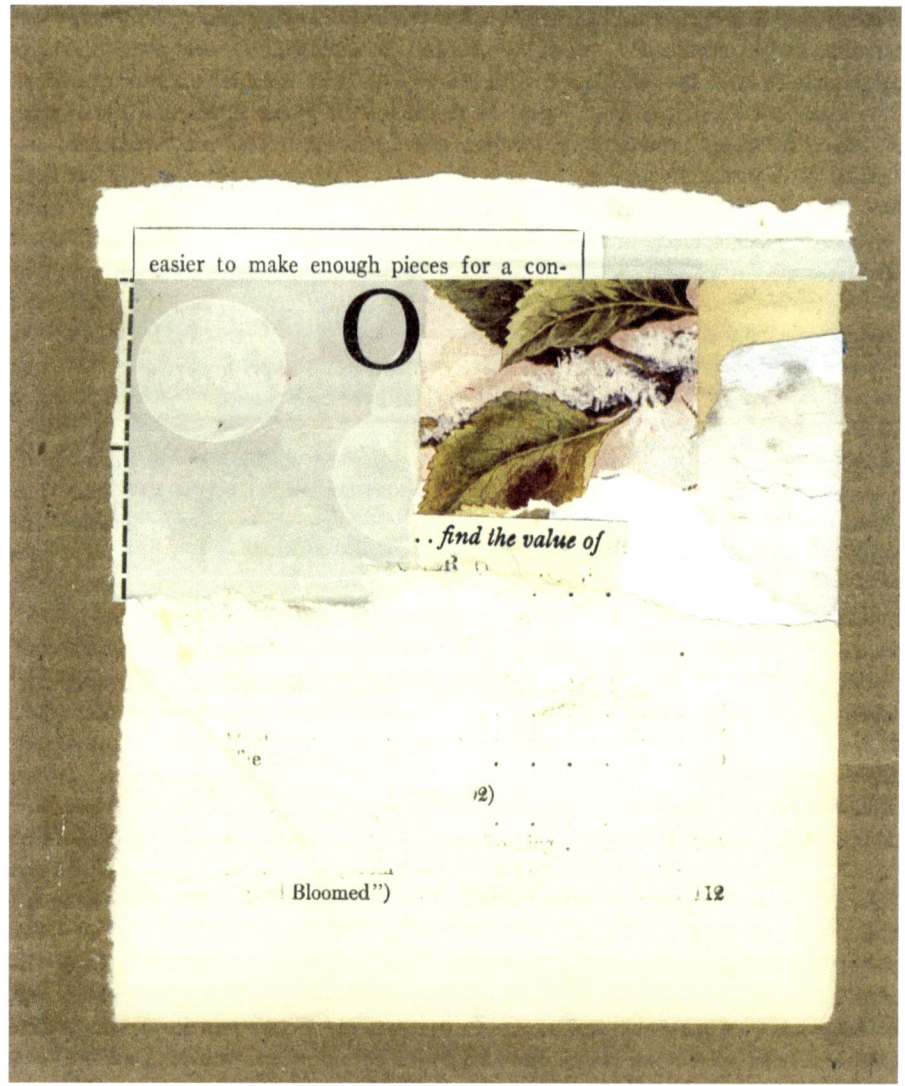

easier to make enough pieces for a con-

O

. . *find the value of*

"e

2)

Bloomed") 12

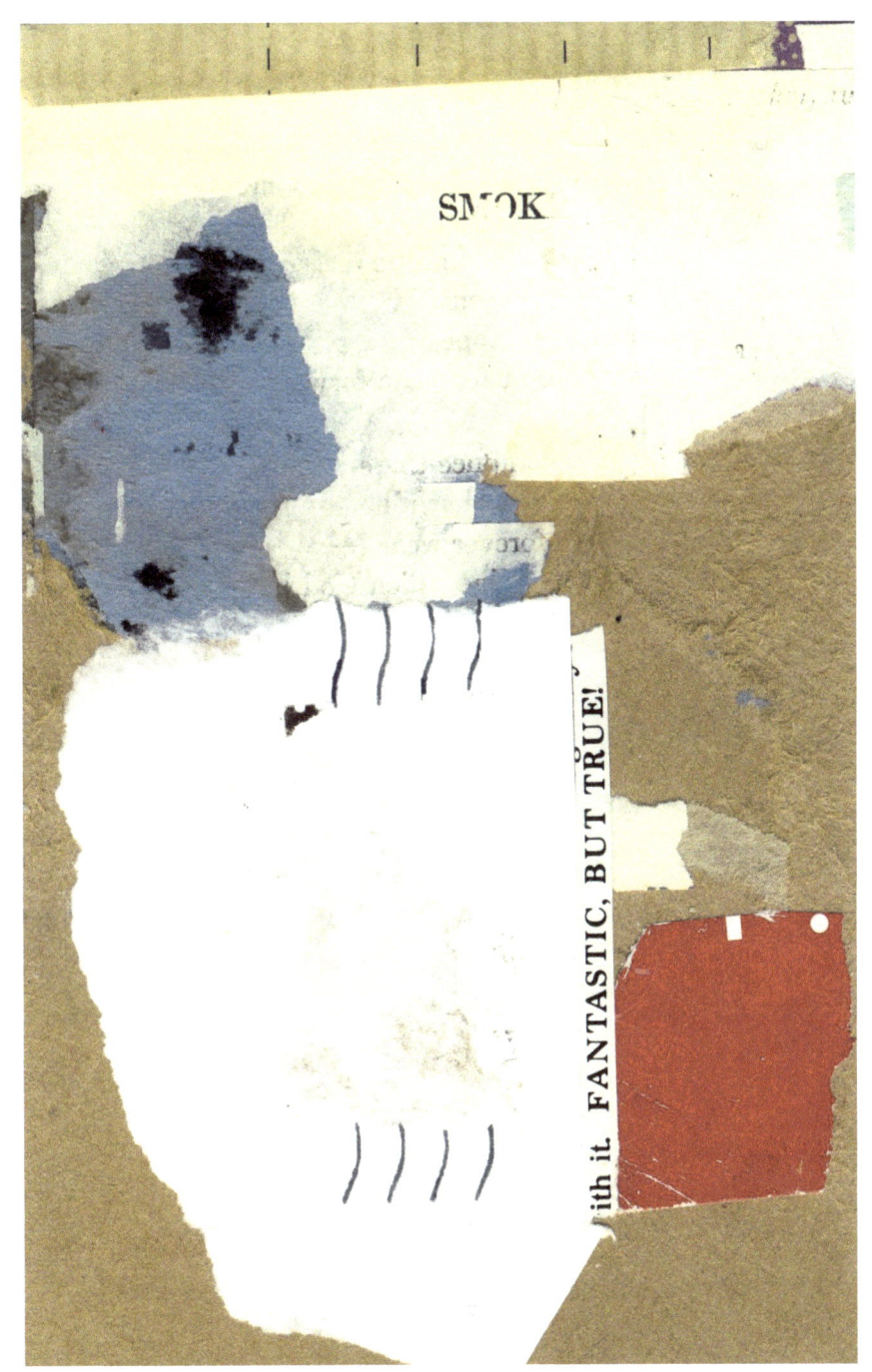

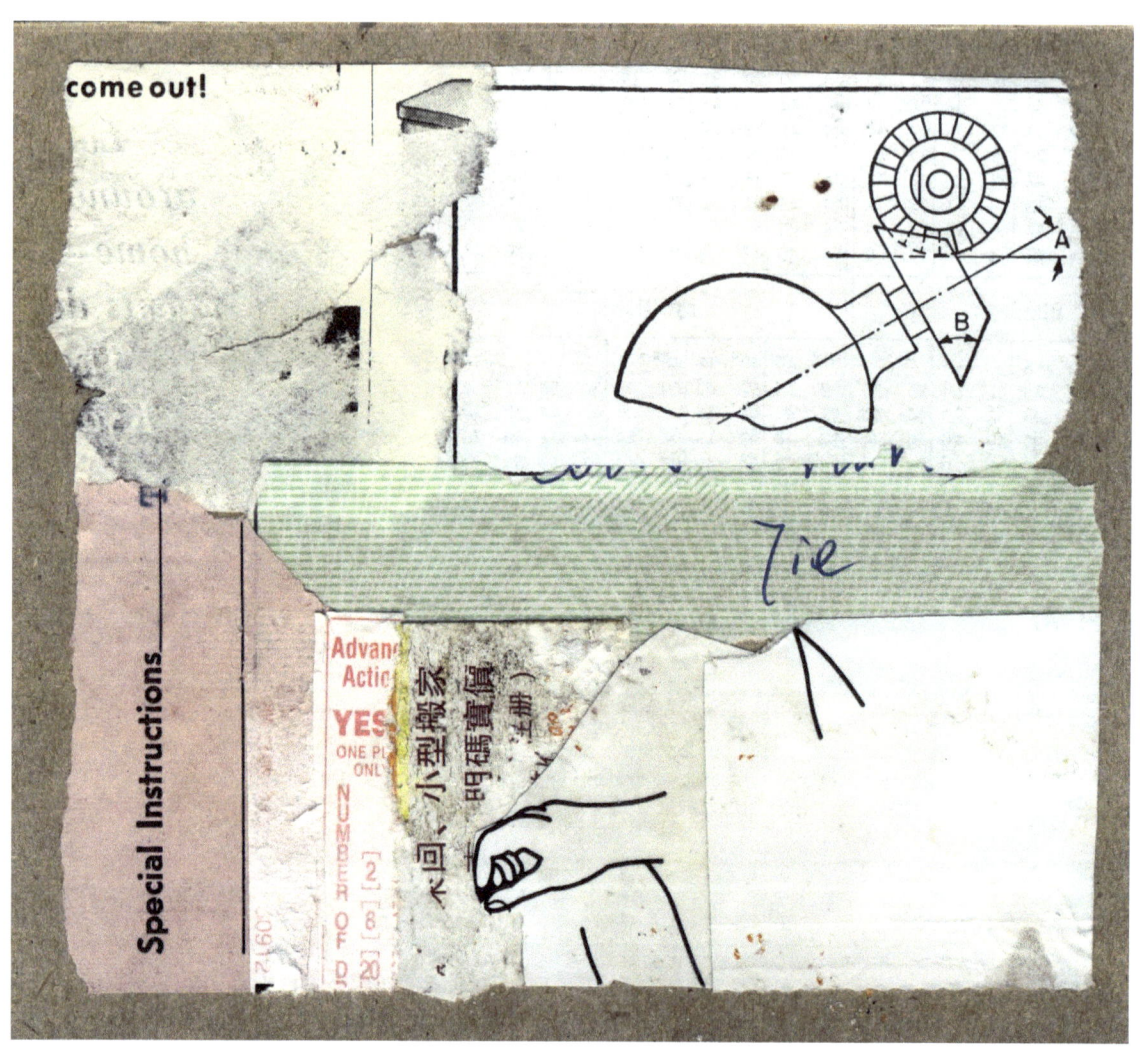

REPONSE URGENTE

thirsty

Stopping at a fountain on the way

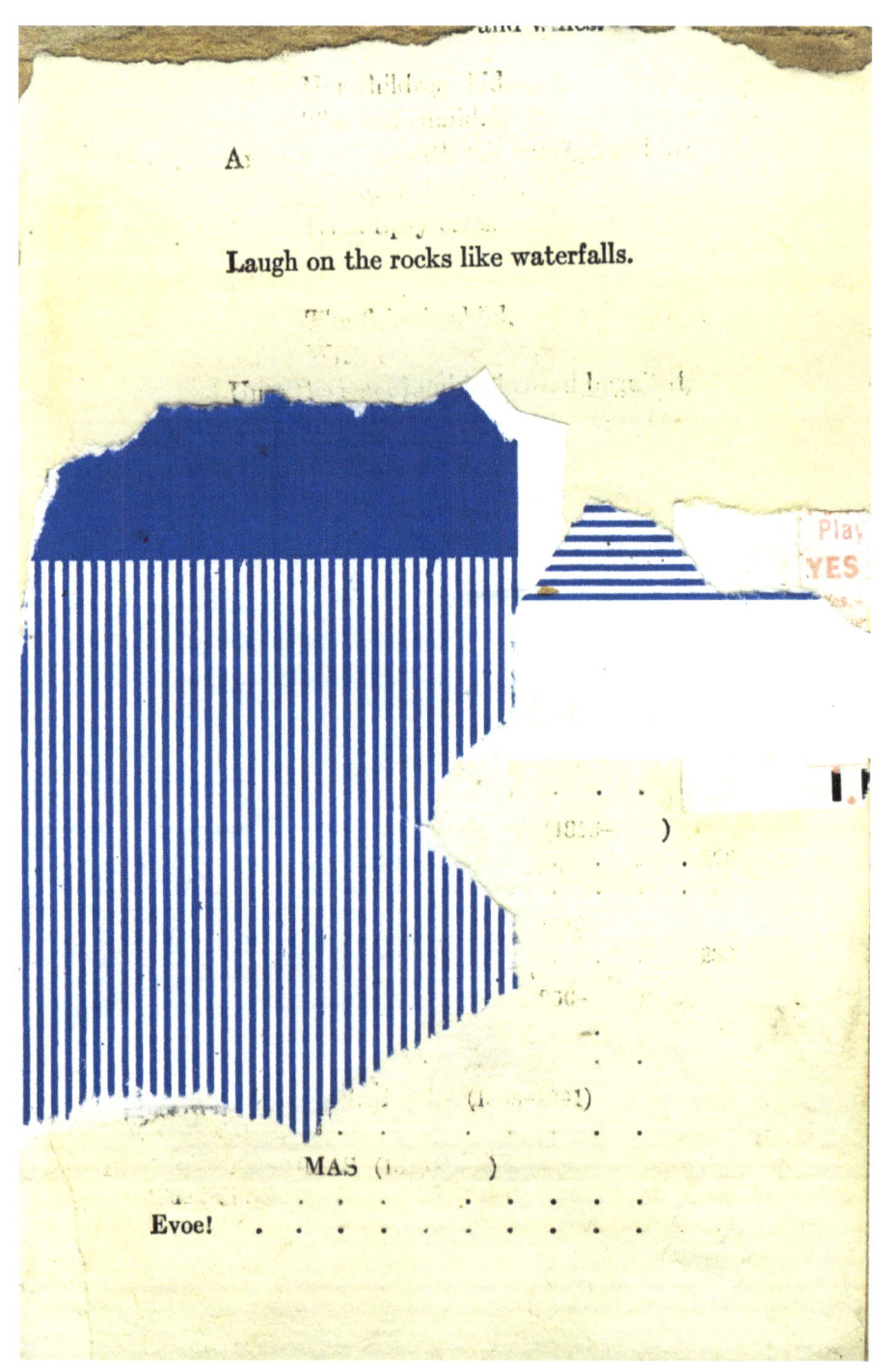

A

Laugh on the rocks like waterfalls.

MAS ( )

Evoe!

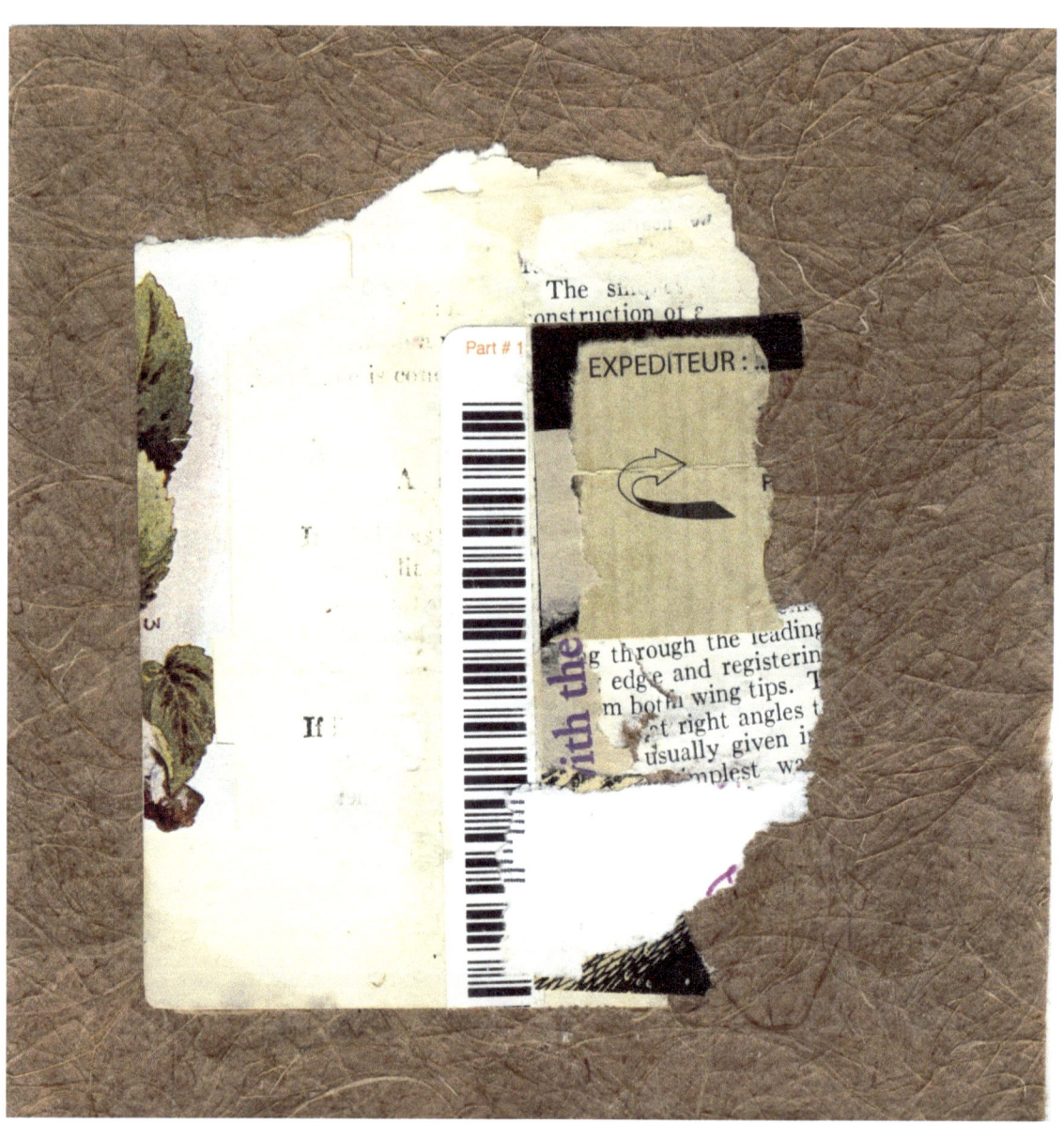

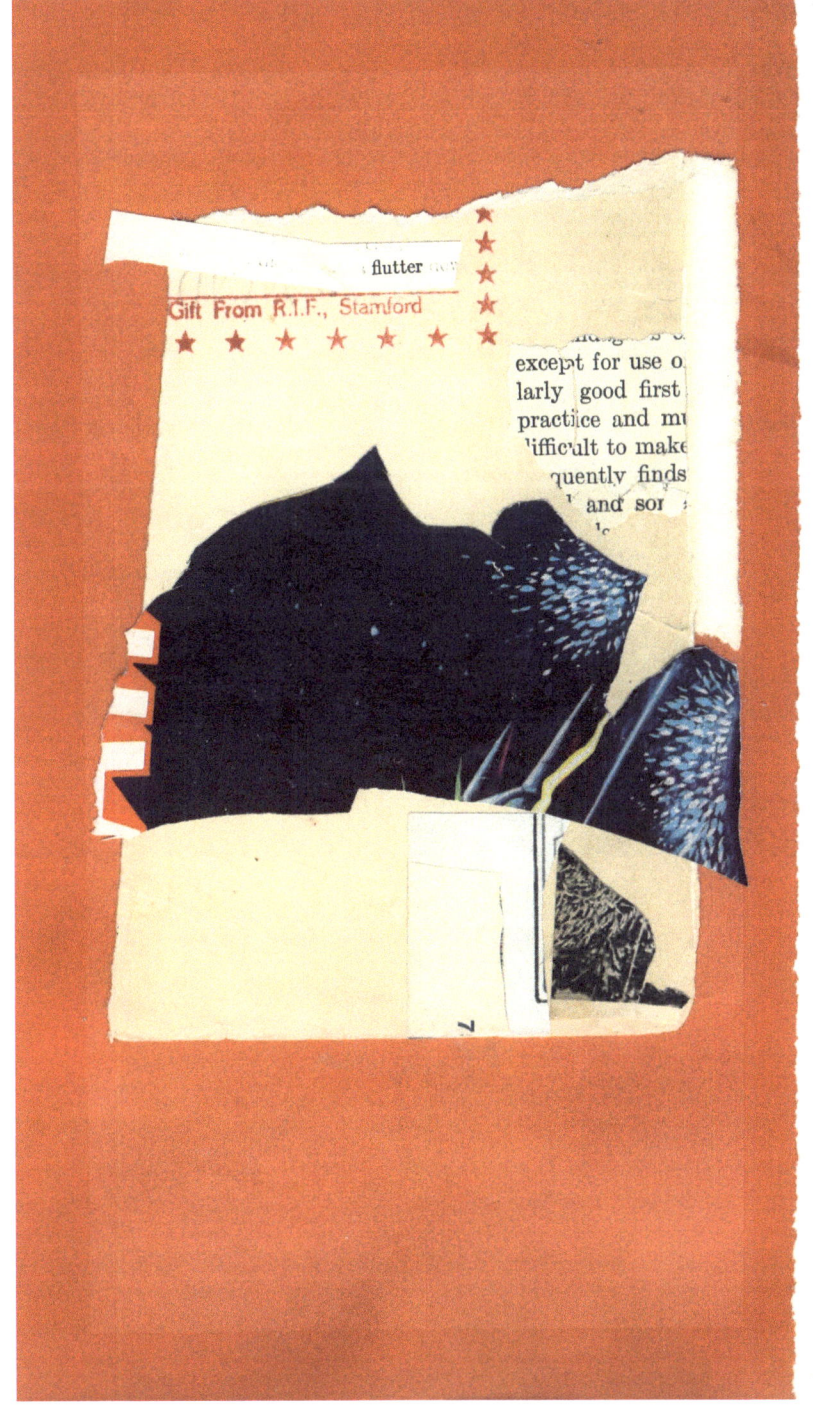

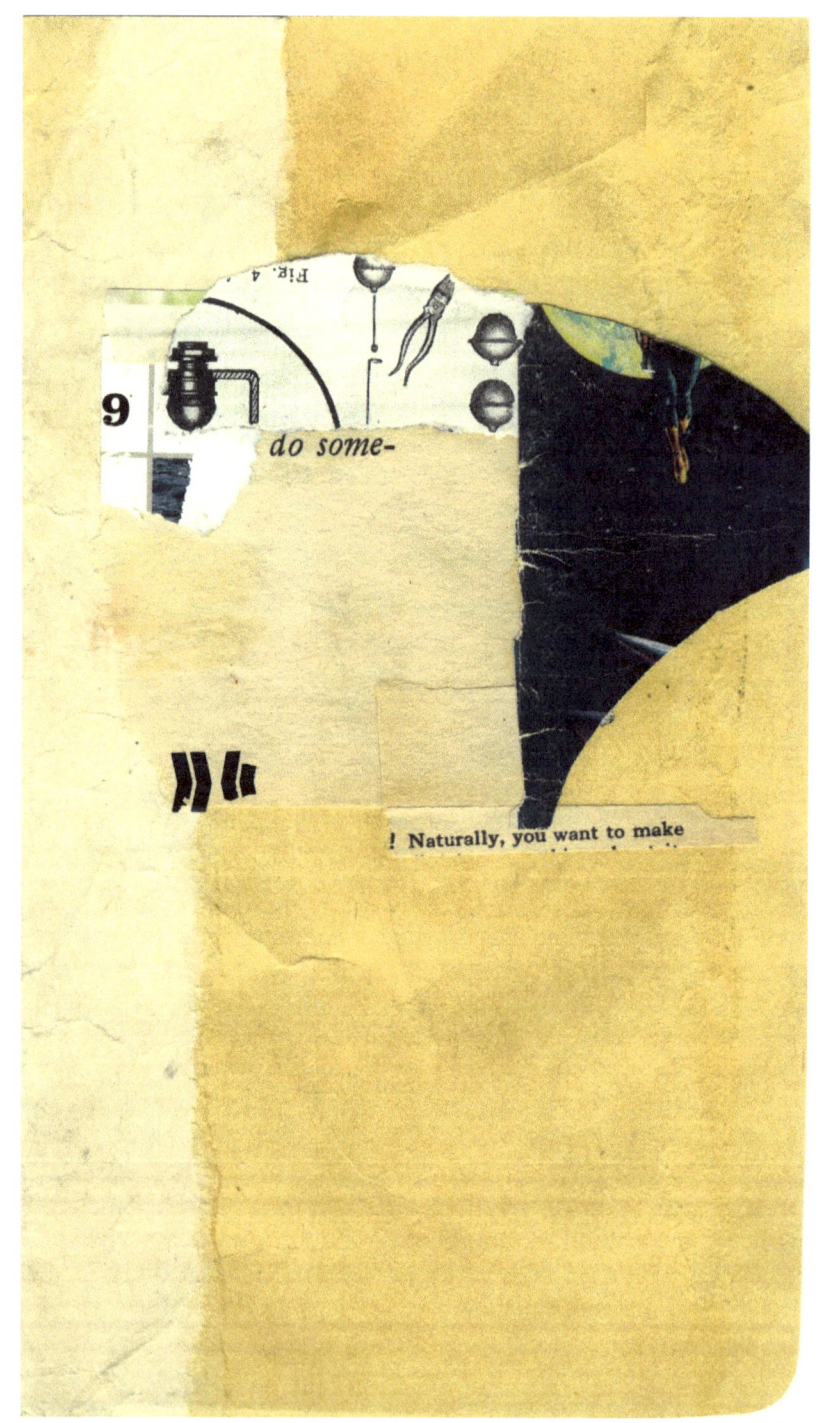

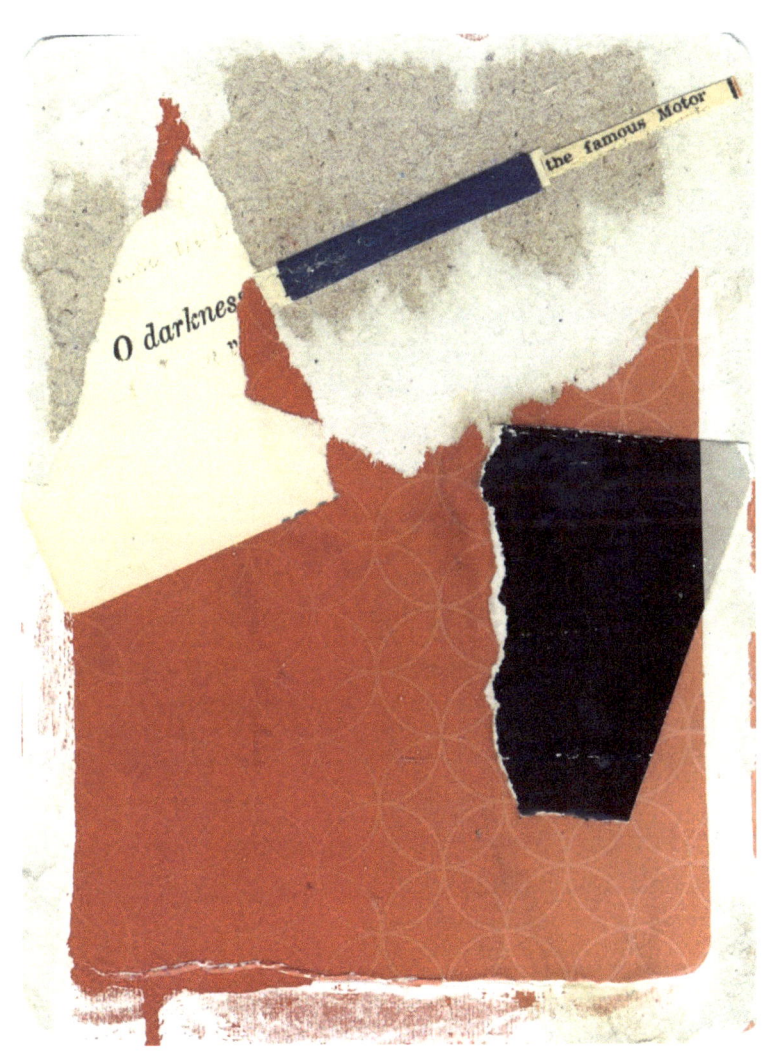

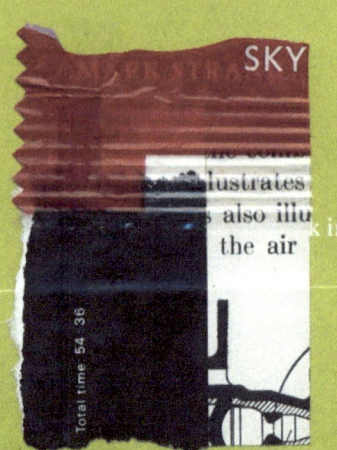

11-17-15

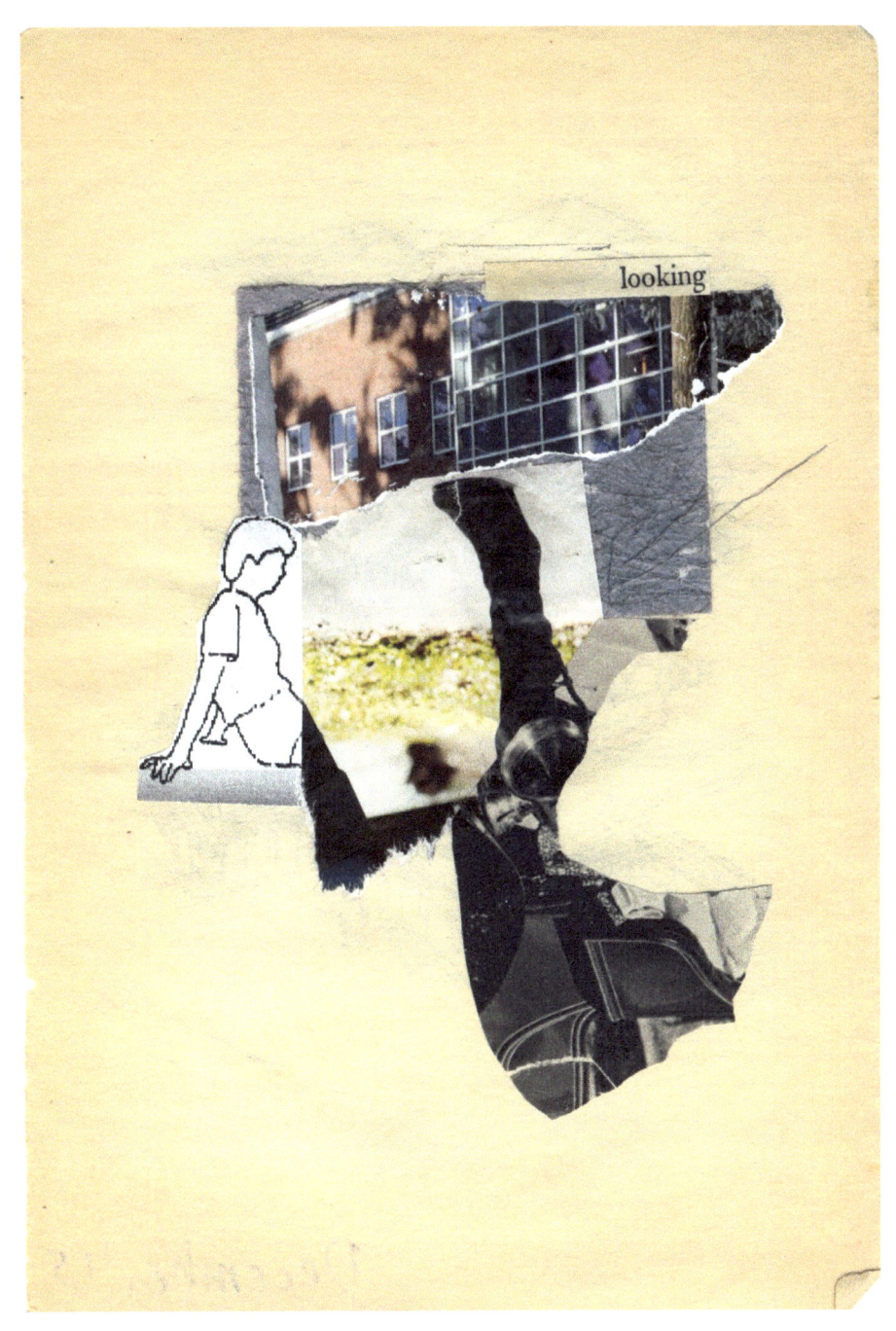

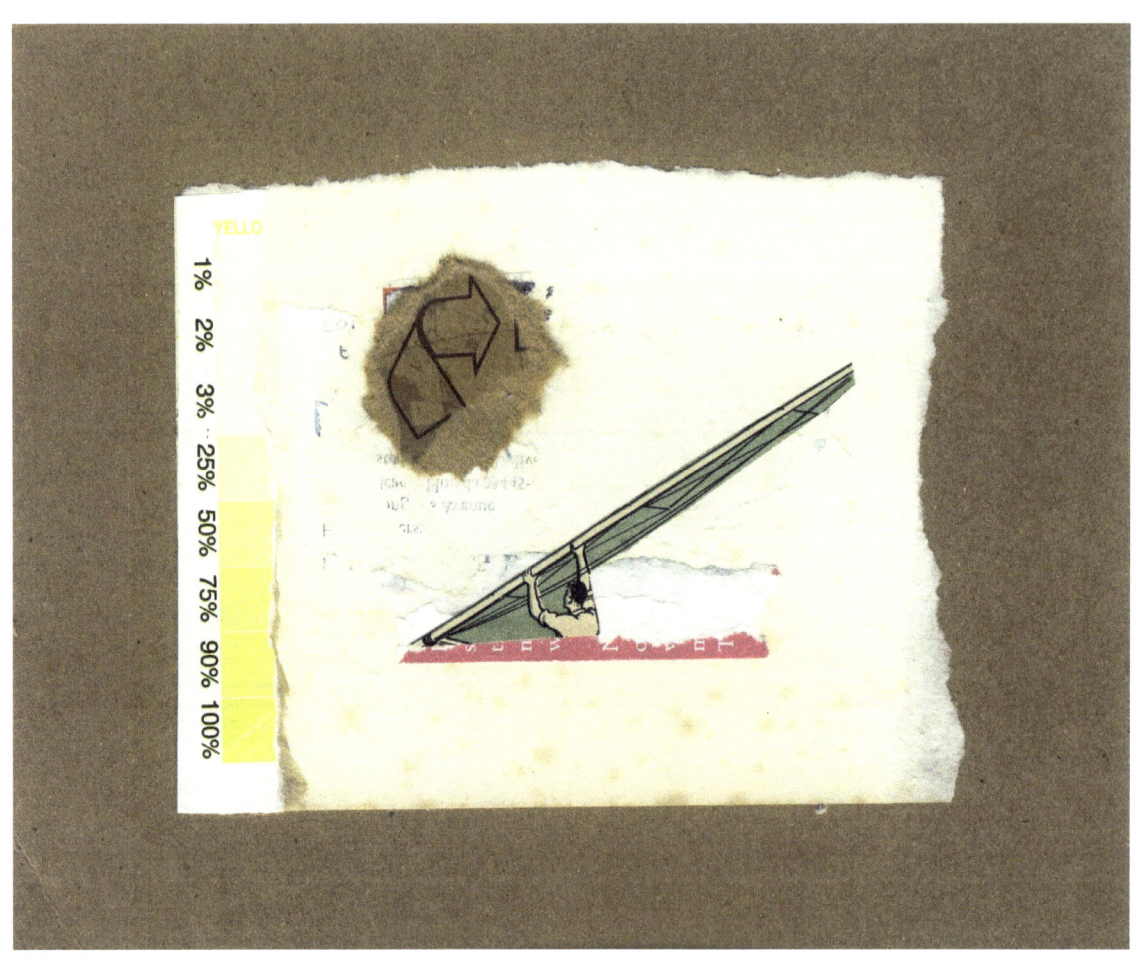

██████████o█ MYSTERY
█o████ █o█ MYSTERY
█o██o████ MYSTERY
█o█o█ MYSTERY
█o████o█ MYSTERY
█o█o█ MYSTERY
███ █o██ MYSTERY
█i███ MYSTERY
████ ████████
MYSTERY ████ ██ ███
██ █████ MYSTERY
████ ███o████ MYSTERY

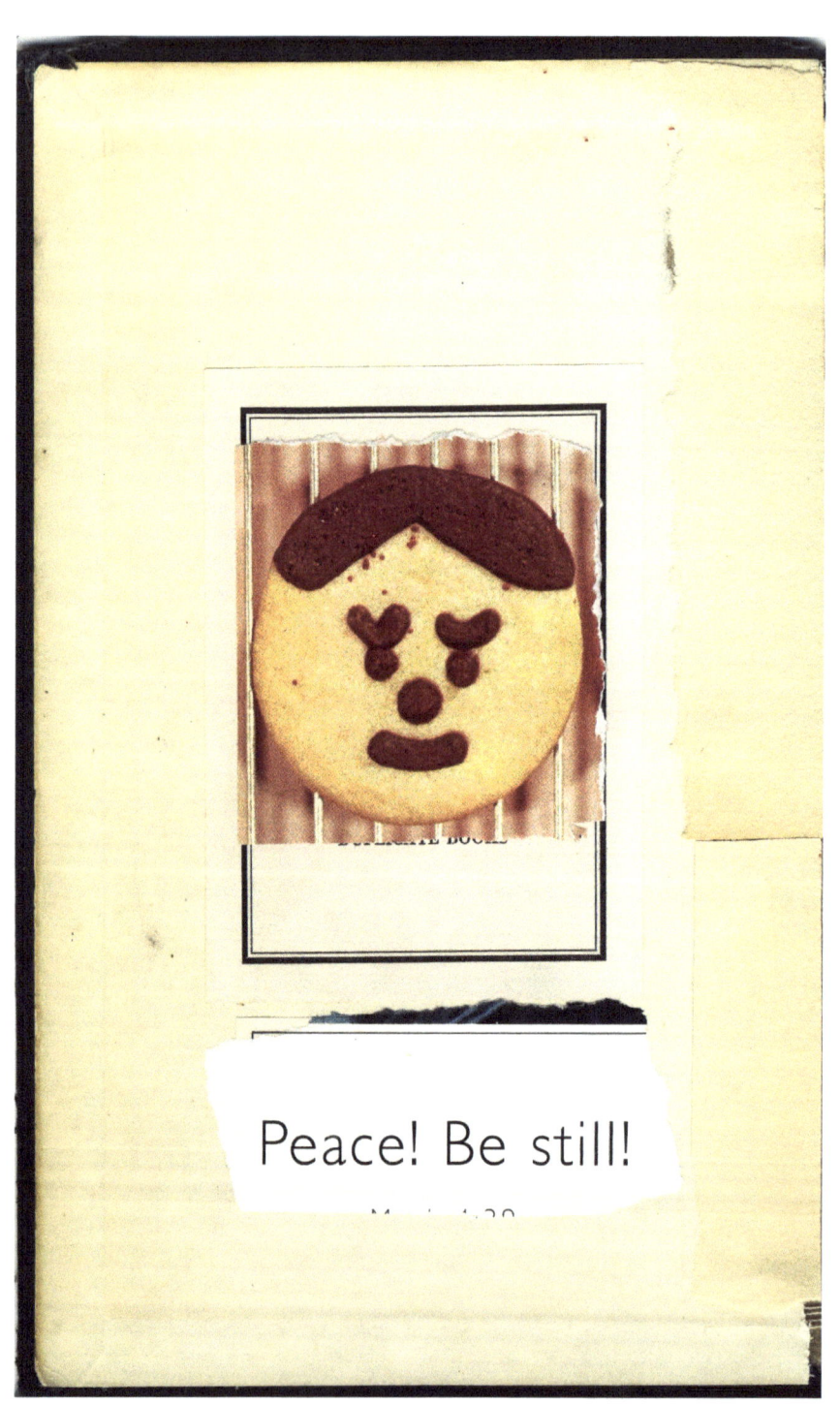

Peace! Be still!

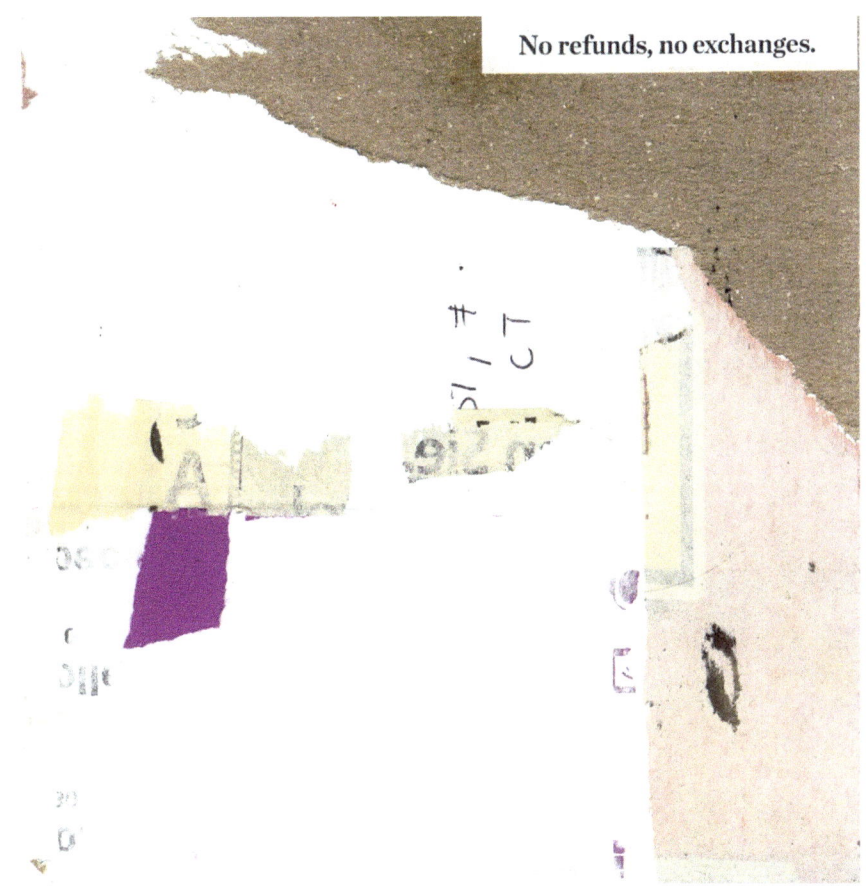

No refunds, no exchanges.

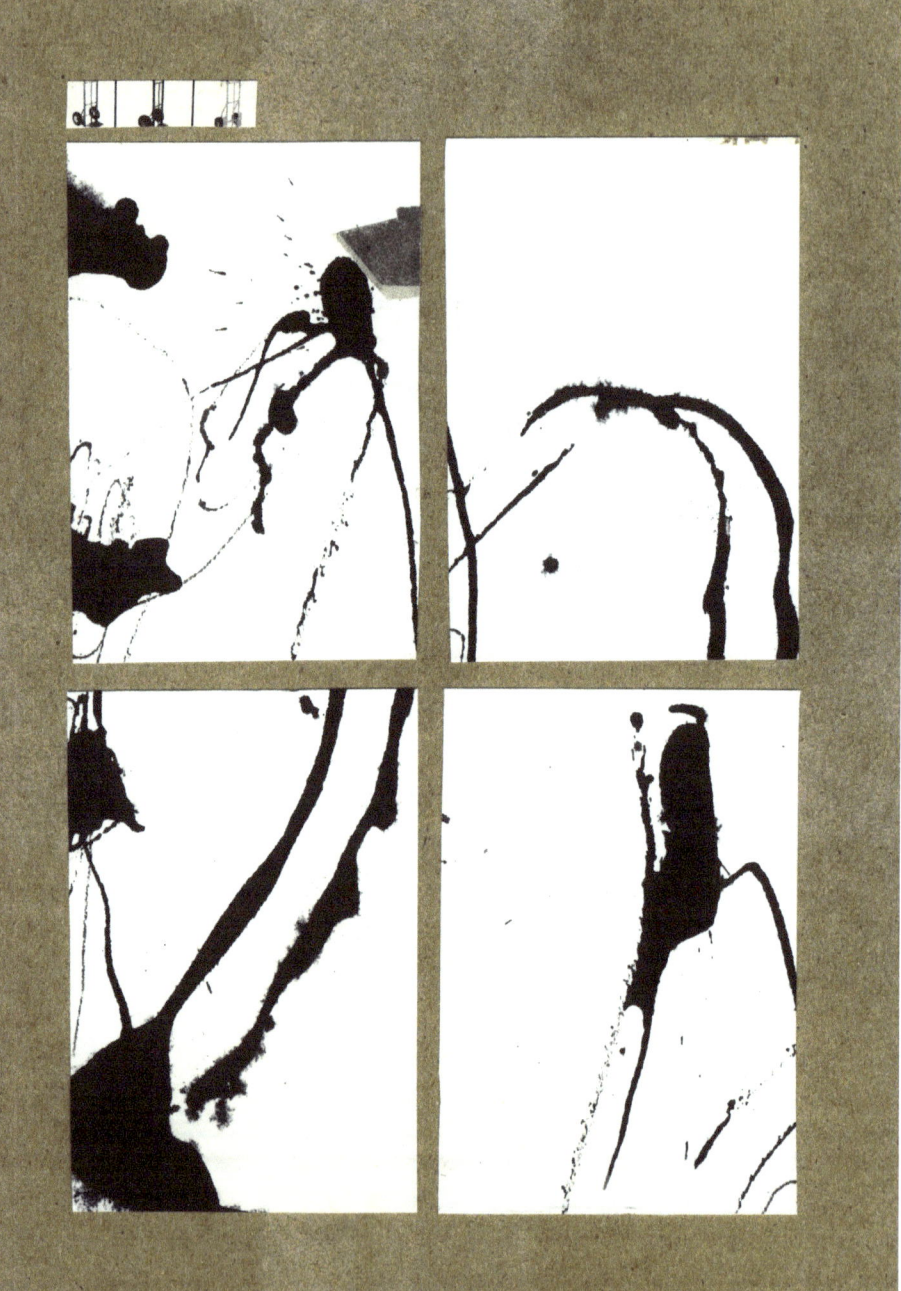

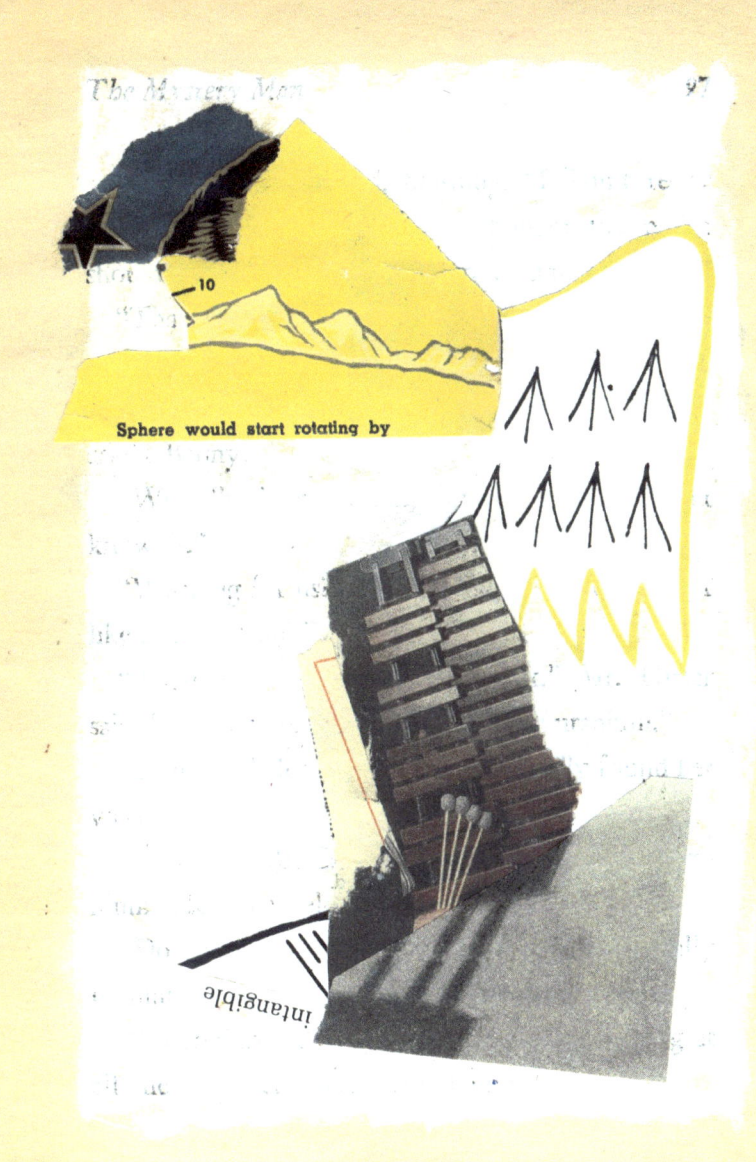

Sphere would start rotating by

intangible

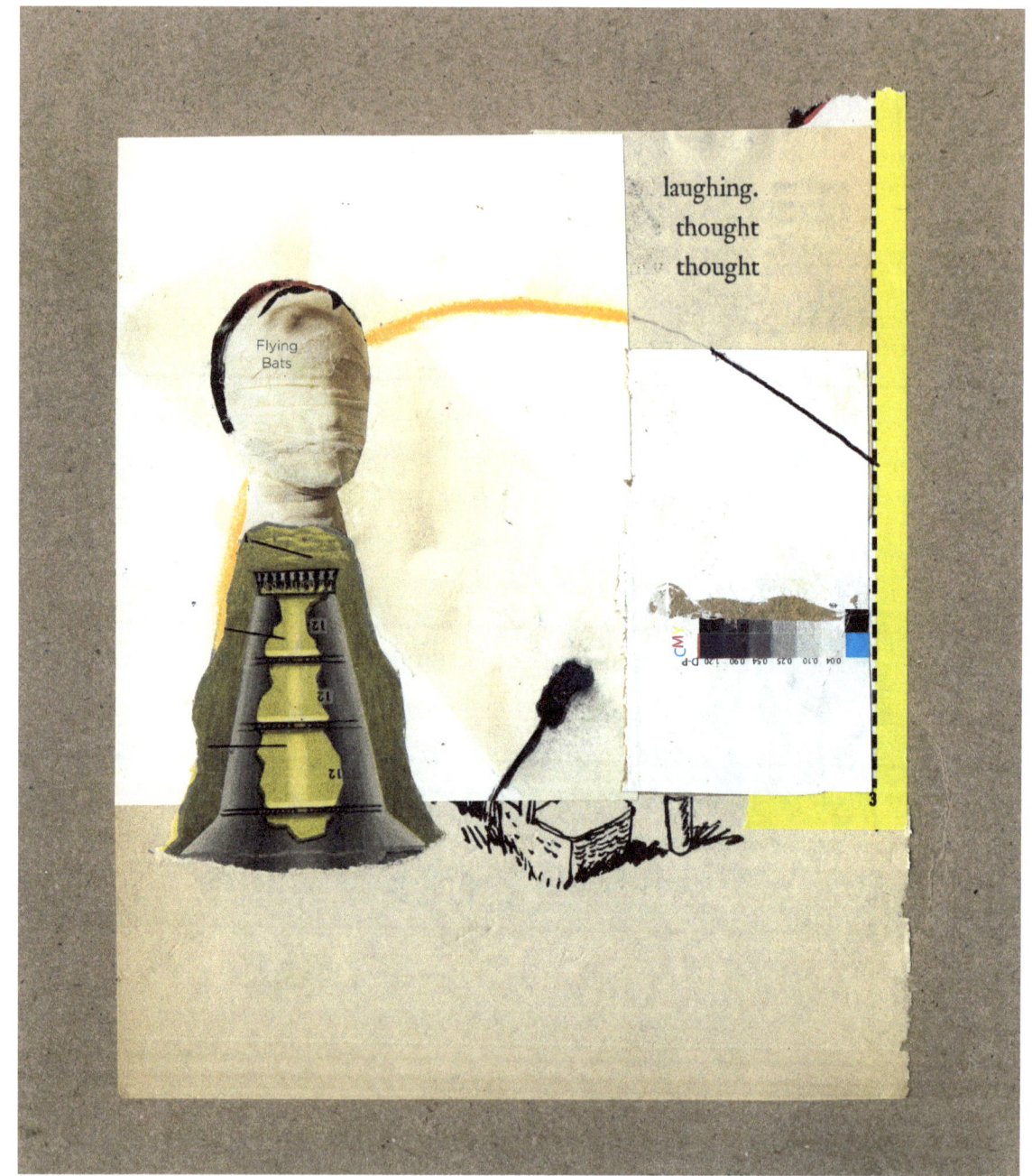

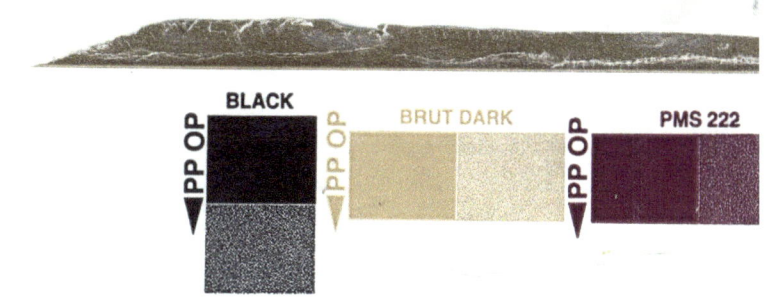

BLACK **BRUT DARK** **PMS 222**

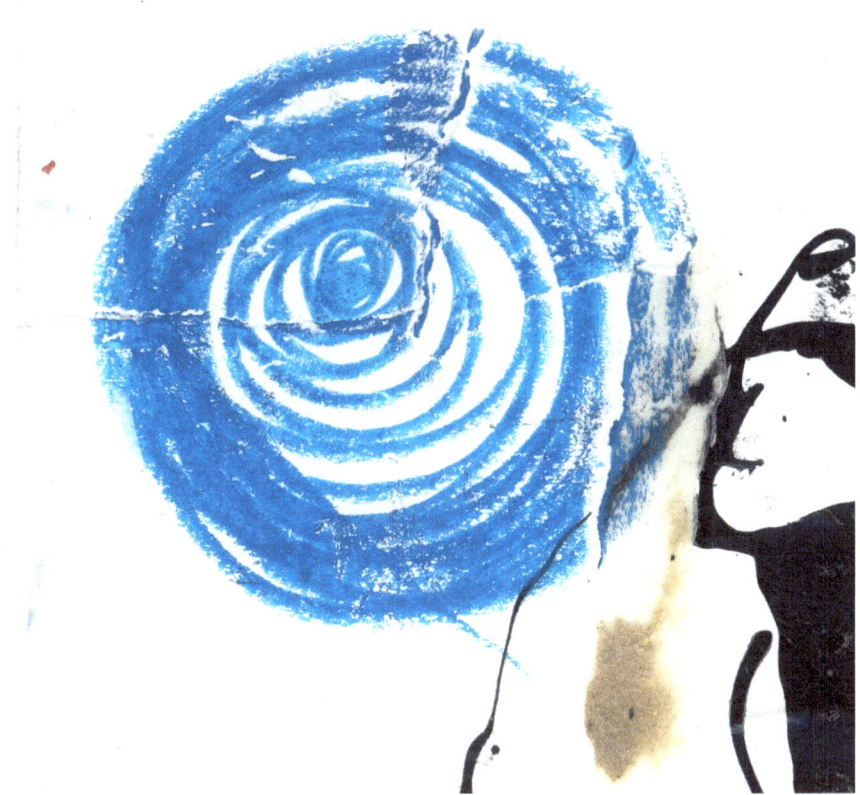

2

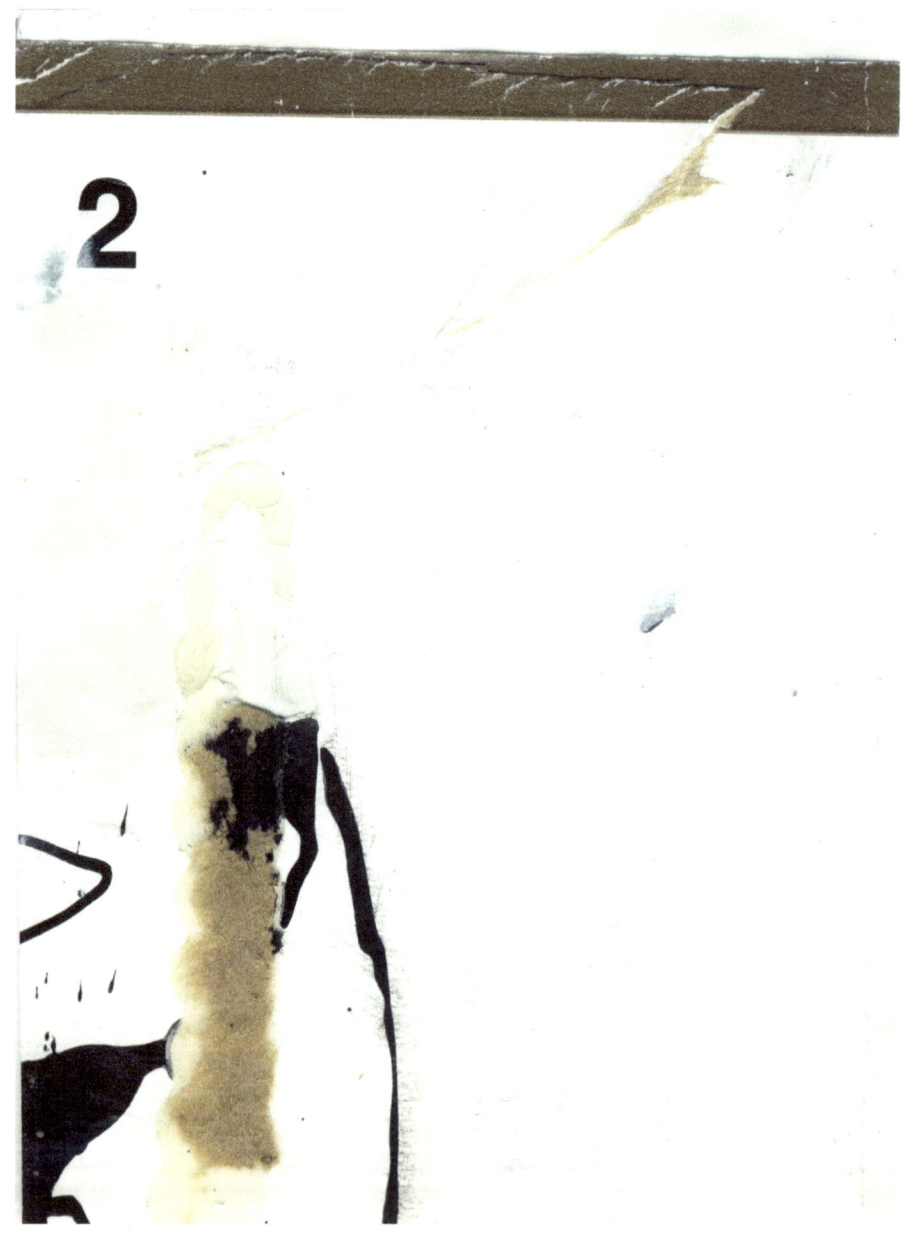

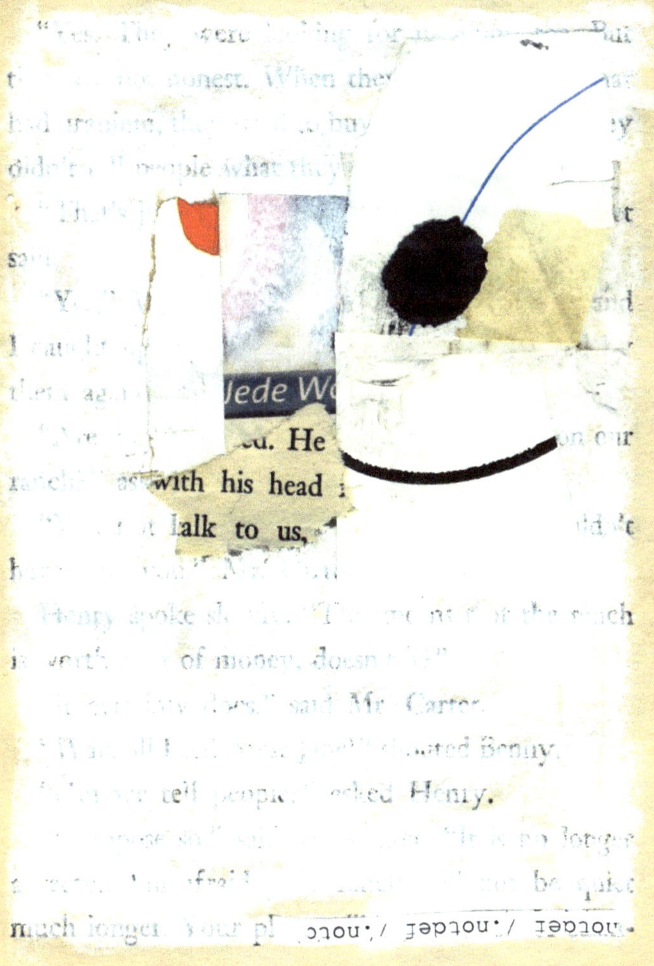
Jede W
with his head
said Mr. Carter.
asked Henry.

CHAPTER 6

Go

We'll have a real

a real

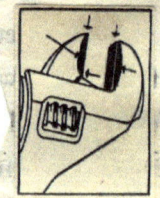

softly opened

CUT

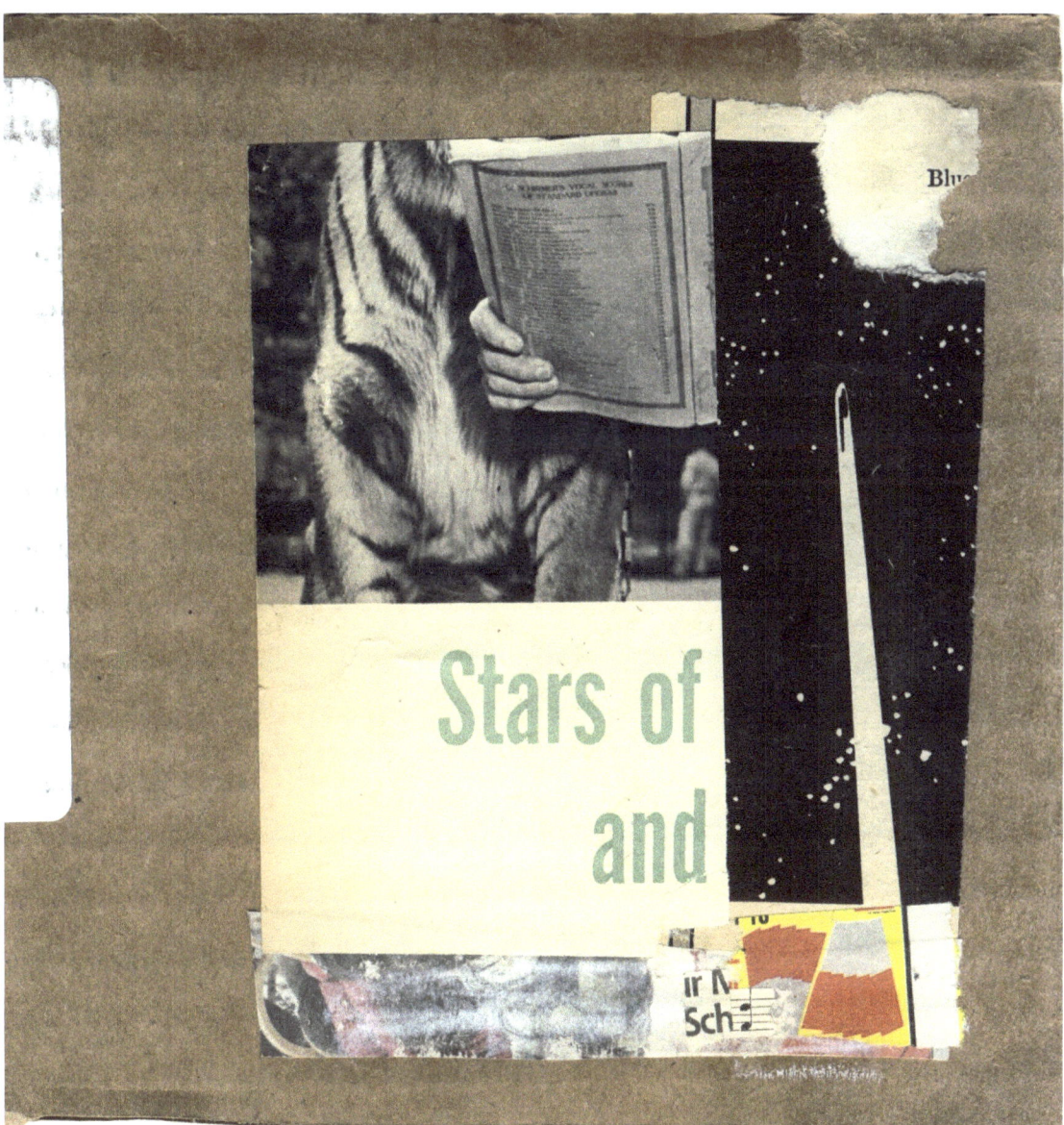

Stars of

and

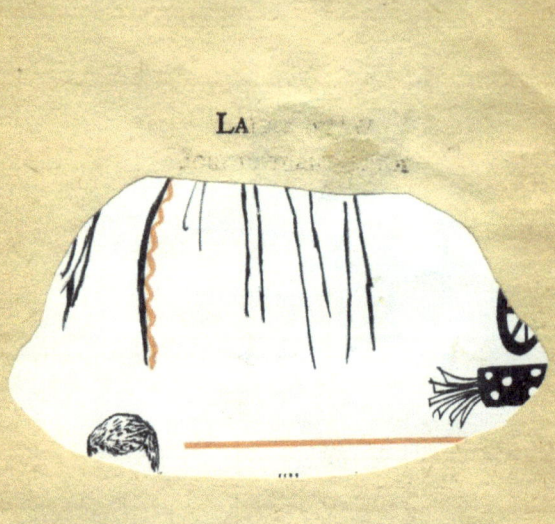

LA

exploring and went back

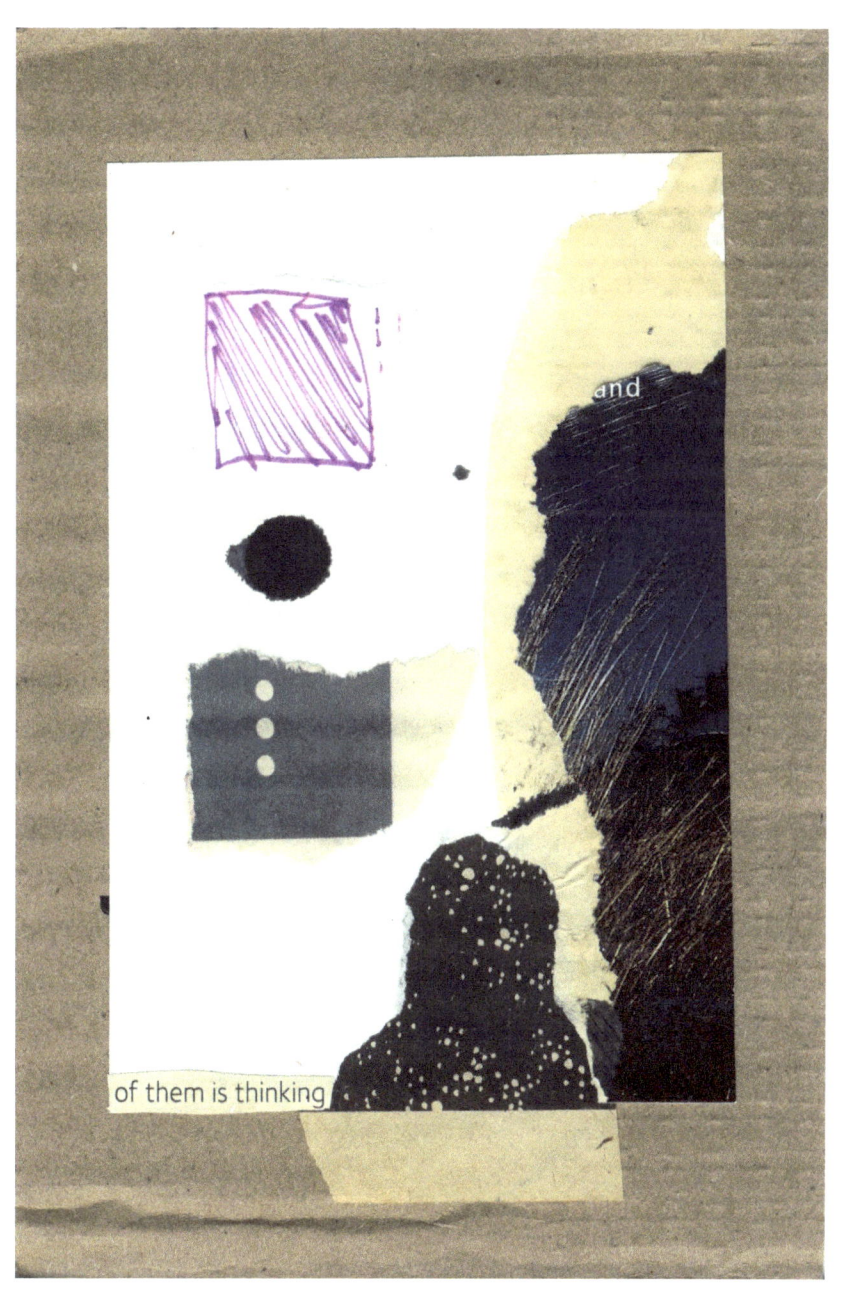

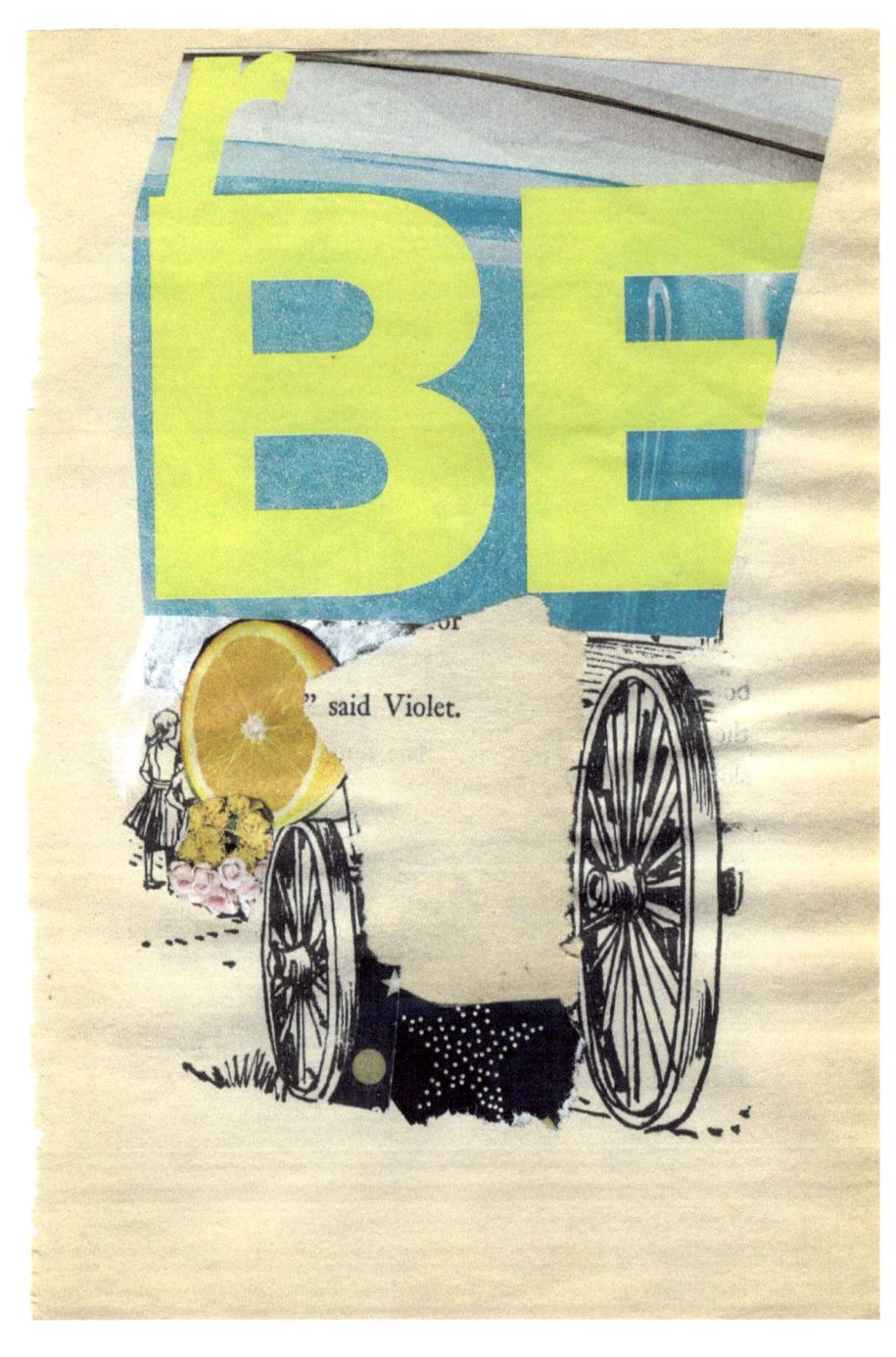

" said Violet.

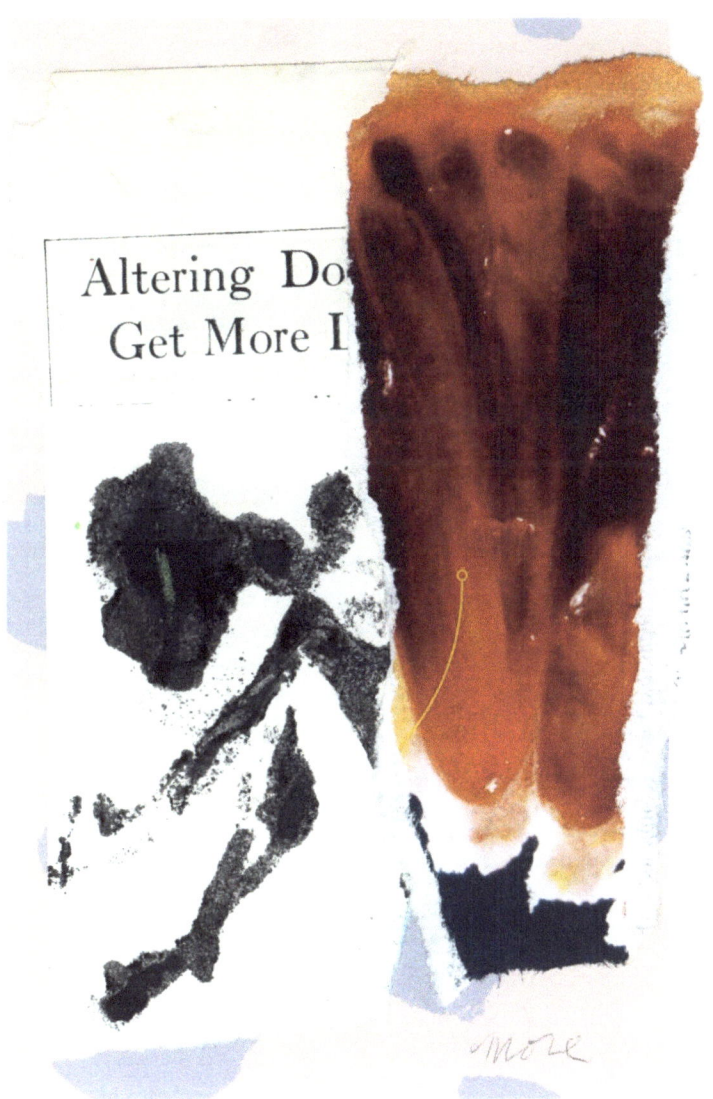

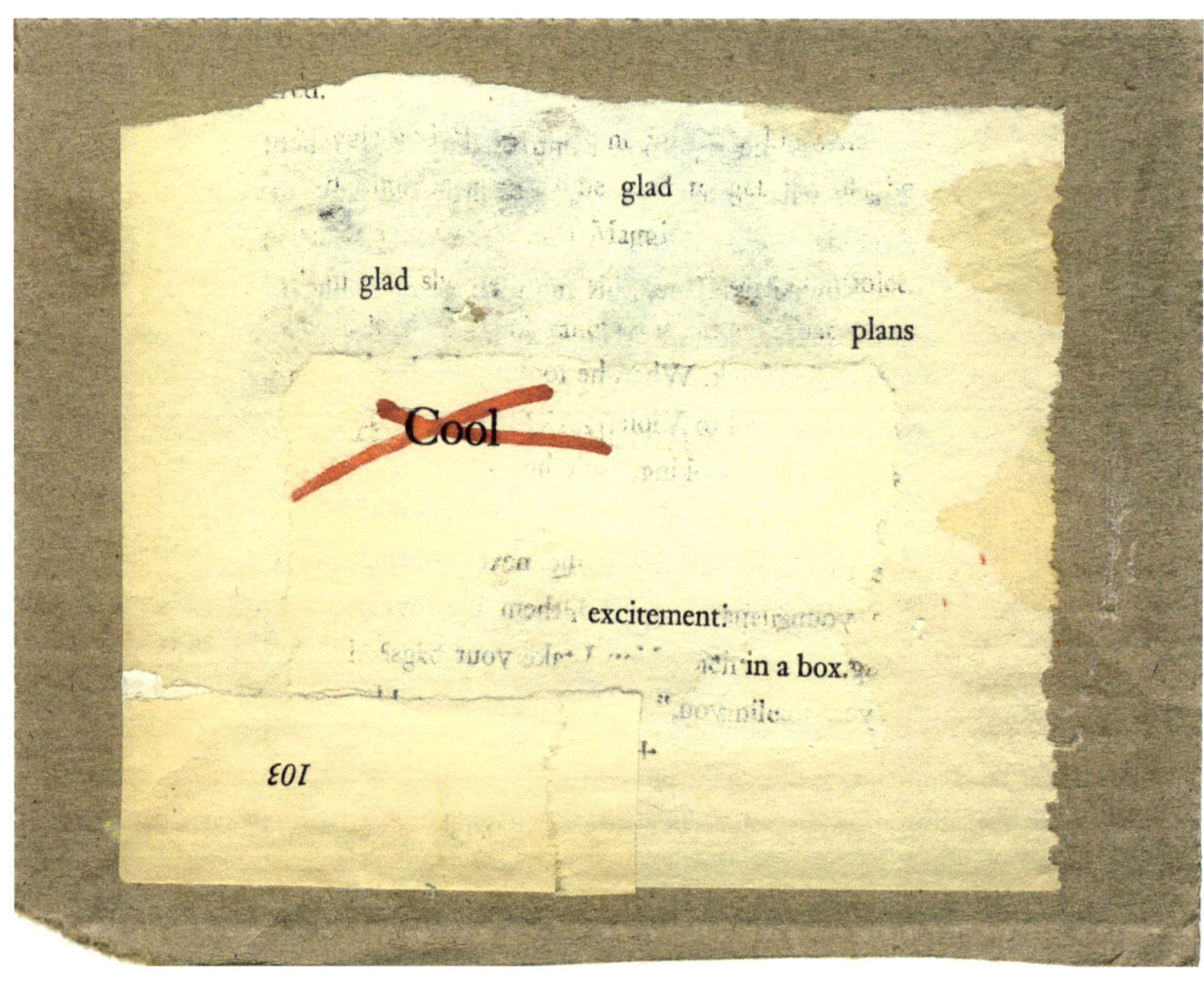

glad

glad

plans

Cool

excitement

in a box.

103

www.ingramcontent.com/pod-product-compliance
Lightning Source LLC
Chambersburg PA
CBHW041301180526
45172CB00003B/920